3. To which note in the chord does the sharp **sign**, flat sign, or natural sign belong? Write the letter-name of the note that has the sharp, flat, or natural before it.

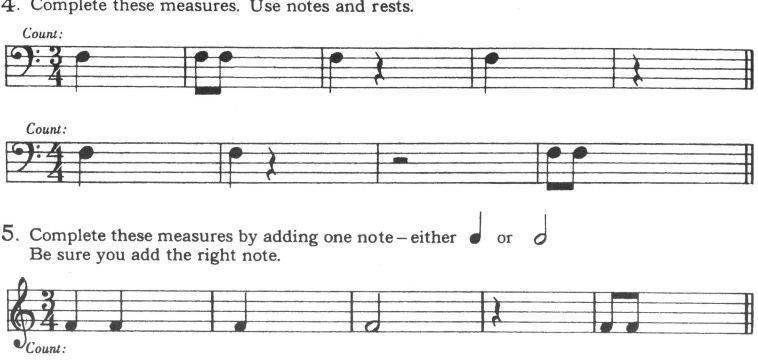

4. Complete these measures. Use notes and rests.

Count:

Count:

5. Complete these measures by adding one note — either ♩ or ♢
   Be sure you add the right note.

Count:

THE INDIAN FLUTE

Almost everyone knows that the North American Indians made drums which they played to celebrate the different ceremonies of Indian life, but did you know that they also made flutes?

Flutes were made of wood hollowed out, and were painted or stained in different colors. You can see that they were not held sideways like the orchestra flute, but were played like whistles. Different notes were formed by closing or opening finger holes bored in the side of the tube.

The Indian, with his love of nature, would be led to play melodies of the great out-doors on his flute—songs of the moon and the stars, of the wind, of running brooks and singing birds; songs of the forest and the plain. Many of these melodies are very beautiful and have been written down so that we can play and sing them.

Name .... Date ....

1. In this story, the missing words are spelled in notes. Write the missing words below the story.

TOMMY AND THE EAGLE

Tommy liked to watch birds in their natural haunts, not _____. He would never take an

_____ from a bird's nest. An eagle built its nest on a cliff by the sea. Tommy crept out to the

_____ of the cliff. He _____ the distance down to a ledge and

_____ carefully over. The _____ eagle was circling over the rocks below.

Tommy climbed back up the _____ of the cliff. The daylight had _____

the tide had _____ from the shore. Tommy about _____ and ran for home.

The missing words are: _____

_____

_____

2. Write in two different places on the treble staff:

Write in two different places on the bass staff:

E	E	C	C	F	F	D	D	G	G	C	C	A	A	B	B

5. Trace and draw eighth rests:

The Eighth-Rest 𝄾 looks like a little flag. It has the same time value as the eighth-note ♪ - only half of a beat, or count.

𝄾 + 𝄾 = 1 count, or beat

𝄾 + ♪ = 1 count, or beat

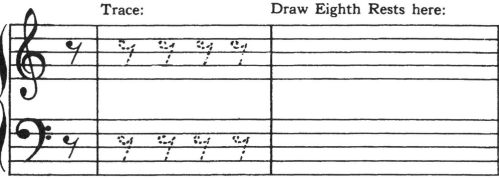

Trace: Draw Eighth Rests here:

6. Write the counts in these measures:

Count:

7. Add notes to complete these measures:

Count:

Count:

THE GUITAR

The guitar has a soft, dreamy quality of tone that makes it especially suitable for accompanying singing.

Sometimes the guitar is used in the modern orchestra, and in the Spanish band it is one of the principle instruments.

The guitar has six strings. The fingerboard is fretted. Tone is produced by plucking the strings.

Name .... Date ....

1. The Jolly Gym Boys are having fun in the gymnasium. Write their names:

Letter-names:

2. Write the letter-names: (Write very neatly.)

3. Write these notes in three different places on the staff:

G	B	D	F	A	C	E

4. Write the letter-names:

Letter-names

4. The Time Signatures have been left out! Put them in. (First, write the counts in each measure and then you will know what the time signature should be.)

THE DOUBLE BASS

Here is a truly huge violin! It is so big that the player has to stand to play it. It is called the Double Bass. The double bass is the largest member of the violin family.

When you look at the long, thick strings of the double bass you know that it has a very low "voice". The double bass plays the lowest tones in orchestra music—the bass notes of the harmony.

The strings are bowed or plucked. Plucked strings are very effective, as the long strings of the double bass vibrate with force, causing each note to "hum".

Name ....   Date ....

1. In this story, the missing words are spelled in notes. Write the missing words below the story.

AT GRANDFATHER'S FARM

Bobby was very busy at grandfather's farm. He chased the cow from the [notes]

field. He gave the chickens their [notes]. He gathered a large [notes] of hickory nuts.

He [notes] the [notes] rabbits some lettuce. He raked up the [notes]

leaves. He made a grinning pumpkin [notes]. He taught the puppy to [notes]

He [notes] apples. Then grandfather called: "Come Bobby! You have done more

than one good [notes] to-day, and it is time you were fast asleep in [notes]"

The missing words are: _____

_____

_____

2. Copy these notes and their letter-names three times:

C   B   A   G

3. Write the letter-names and then copy three times:

Letter-names:

5. Each measure is unfinished. Add notes to complete each measure. Then write the counts:

Count:

Count:

Count:

6. Complete these measures by adding rests. Then write the counts:

Count:

Count:

THE CLARINET

The clarinet is a most interesting musical instrument. It has a rich, mellow tone that is very expressive—sometimes it is almost conversational. The volume of the tone can be varied, from the very softest sound to the very loudest!

The clarinet is an important instrument in the orchestra where it plays melodies as well as harmonies. You will probably see three clarinets in the symphony orchestra. In the concert band, however, or in the military band, you will notice a large number of clarinets. This is because the clarinet occupies the place in the band that the violin occupies in the orchestra.

Name .... Date ....

1. Trace the sharp, flat, and natural signs and the notes. (Notice how the sharp, flat, and natural sign is placed when it is on a line and when it is in a space.)

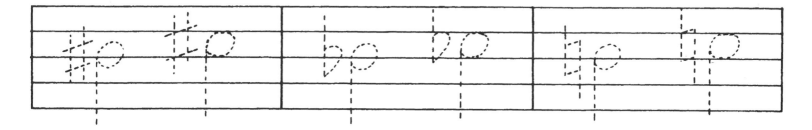

2. Draw the sharp, flat, and natural signs and notes in Question 1 here:

3. Write the letter-names of these notes:

G♯

4. Write each note on the treble staff and also on the bass staff.

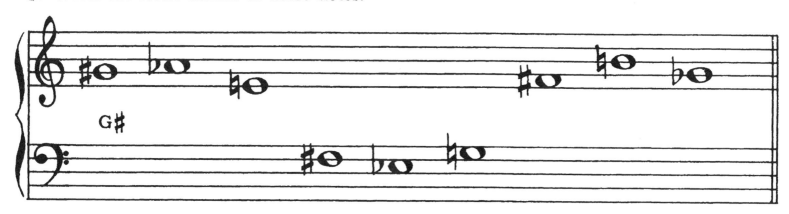

G♯   B♭   E♮   D♯   F♮   A♭   C♯

3. Put in bar lines:

THE LUTE

The boy playing the lute is probably singing a Christmas Carol.

The lute is an ancient instrument that was very important and popular years ago. Sometimes we find it mentioned in old songs. It was used a great deal for accompanying singers. It was also an important instrument in the orchestra in olden days. There were many different varieties of lutes, some being very large and having many strings.

The lute was played by plucking the strings with the fingers of the right hand, while the left hand fingers stopped the strings at the frets to form the different notes.

Name .... Date ....

1. In this story, the missing words are spelled in notes. Write the missing words below the story.

THE NAUGHTY LITTLE BABE

The naughty little [notes] would not [notes] good, not for his mother, or his

nurse, or even his [notes] A [notes] flew by and the [notes]

cried for it. He threw his nice, old, [notes] elephant on the floor. When nurse tried to

wash his [notes] he hid his [notes] in his chubby hands. "You naughty little

[notes] ," said nurse. "Perhaps you are sleepy!" Big tears rolled down the babe's

[notes] So they put him to [notes] and when he awoke he was no longer a

naughty little [notes] !

The missing words are: _____

_____

_____

2. Write the letter-names of these notes:

Letter-
names:

3. The bar-lines have been left out! Put them in. Be sure you have the right number of **beats** in each measure.

This upper figure
tells you
how many counts
there are
in each measure.

Look!

Look!

THE TROMBONE

Here is the trombone, a brass instrument that can be played as smoothly as a violin! The trombone is different from all other horns in that it is played by means of a sliding tube, which the player draws longer for lower notes and shorter for higher notes. In this way the trombone player adjusts the length of the tube to form the different notes, and it is this feature that gives the trombone its lovely, legato quality of tone.

The trombone has great beauty of tone. It is especially noble and expressive. In volume it has a very wide range, from the softest, most delicate **pianissimo** to the loudest, most majestic **fortissimo.**

You will see and hear the trombone in both orchestras and bands.

Name .... Date ....

1. Write these words in notes on the treble staff and on the bass staff. In this way you will write each word twice — once on the treble staff and once on the bass staff. Use whole notes.

| F E E | A D D | B E G | C A B | A G E |

| B A B E | F A C E | B E A D | F A D E |

2. Write the counts in these measures:

Count:

Count:

Count:

Count:

3. Write the counts in these measures:

Count:

Count:

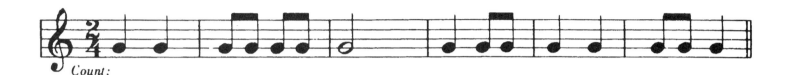
Count:

4. Write four measures of $\frac{4}{4}$ time here:

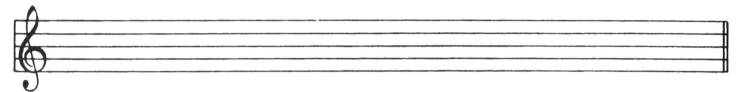

THE FLUTE

Flutes of various kinds have been used in different countries of the world as far back as the history of music can take us.

To-day the flute is used chiefly in orchestras. The flute has one of the most beautiful "voices" of the whole orchestra. The tone is sweet and gentle and the higher notes are brilliant.

The flute is held sideways, and is played by blowing across an opening near the end of the tube. The different notes are formed by opening and closing the finger holes and keys, and also by blowing with varying force — the greater the air pressure in the tube, the higher the sound will be.

The great composer, Mozart, wrote an opera called "The Magic Flute."

Name .... Date ....

1. In this story, the missing words are spelled in notes. Write the missing words below the story. There is a place there for them.

THE BUSY LITTLE BEE

The missing words are: _____

_____

_____

2. Write the letter-names of these notes:

·1 Read what the note is saying:

   "My name is Eighth-Note. I get only half-of-one count. When my twin brother goes with me

the two of us together get one count: ♪ ♪

When we are together we usually join hands: ♫

5. Write a line of eighth notes here. Join the stems of some of them.

6. Write a four-beat   a two-beat note here: a one-beat note here: a note that gets only half of
    note here: one beat here:

7. Write the counts in these measures:

Count:

THE BANJO

The happy-looking sailor is playing a banjo. Have you ever heard the cheerful "plink-a-plunk" of the banjo? Its music is so rhythmic and jolly.

The banjo has a round, drum-like body; it has four (or five) strings, and a long fingerboard with frets. (Frets are little bars across the fingerboard which mark the different notes.) Tone is produced by plucking the strings, while the different notes are formed by the fingers of the left hand stopping the strings at the frets.

There is a song written by Stephen Foster, about Alabama, a banjo, and a girl whose name is mentioned in the title of the song. Can you name the song?

BOOK ONE
THEORY PAPER 5

Name ....   Date ....

1. The Jolly Gym Boys are having fun in the gymnasium. Can you write their names?

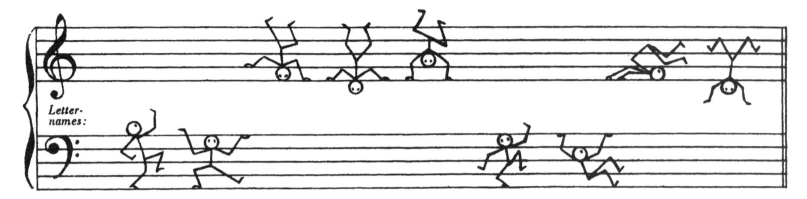

2. Write the letter-names of these notes:

3. Write these notes:

F A C E	C A G E	E D G E	B A B E

4. Read about the happy-looking rests:

The whole-rest is an acrobat — he hangs from the line. For this, he gets 4 counts.

The half-rest is not quite so clever — he sits on the line. He gets 2 counts.

The quarter-rest looks something like a bird flying sideways. Just 1 count for the quarter rest.

5. How many counts does each rest get? Write the number beneath the rest.

6. Write the counts in these measures:

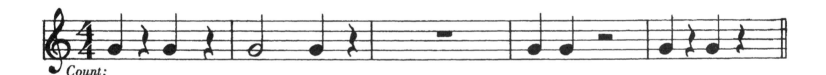

THE VIOLIN

The violin is a very popular instrument. It has a lovely, expressive, singing tone. It is usually accompanied by the piano.

The violin is the most important instrument in the orchestra. In the symphony orchestra you will notice that there are about twenty-five or thirty violins!

The violin has four strings, and tone is produced by drawing the bow across the strings while the fingers of the left hand stop the strings to form the different notes. (You know, the shorter the string, the higher the tone it will give, the longer the string, the lower the tone.) Sometimes the strings are plucked by the fingers. This gives a short, detached sound, which is an interesting contrast to the tone of the bowed notes.

Name .... Date ....

1. Trace:

Draw a brace, a treble clef and bass clef here:

2. Copy these notes and their letter-names:

Copy here   and here   and here.

G A B C

Copy here   and here   and here.

F E D C

3. Write the letter-names of these notes and you will find that the letters spell words:

Letter-names:

5. Write the counts in these measures:

THE HARP

The harp is one of the oldest musical instruments. The beautiful harp shown here is the one we use today. This harp has 47 strings. The C strings are colored red, and the F strings are colored blue, so that the player can easily distinguish the different strings. (The piano and organ have white keys and black keys for the same reason.) The harp has seven pedals which are used to change the pitch of the strings—one pedal for all the C's, another for all the D's, and so on. This is so that the player can change the tuning of the harp when he wishes to play in a different key. Tone is produced by plucking the strings.

Look for the harp at the symphony concert, and listen to its lovely sweeping chords and arpeggios.

Name .... Date ....

1. Trace the piano keyboard and blacken the black keys. Print the letter-names on the white keys.

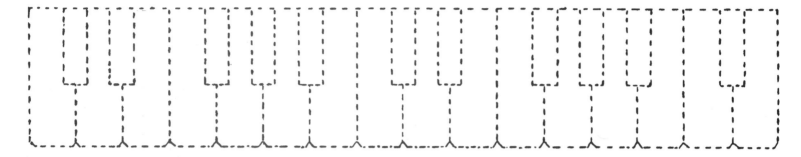

2. Write the letter-names of these notes:

3. Copy the notes in question 2:

4. Write these notes:

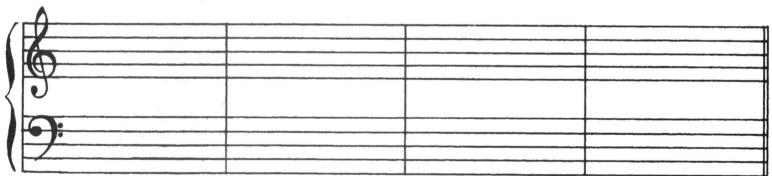

| G | C | A | E | D | B | F | Two different G's | Two different A's | Two different F's |

4. Write the counts in these measures:

THE ORGAN

You have often heard the organ played at church. Perhaps you have wondered at its powerful sound. Have you noticed that although the organ has great volume of tone ,it can also be play-ed very softly?

The organ in the picture has three keyboards, called manuals. Organs have from two to five manuals. There is also a pedal keyboard which is played by the feet. Besides this, the organ has a large number of stops which are used to give different effects of tone.

You can readily understand that it is possible to get an almost endless variety of tone from the organ!

Name .... Date ....

1. Trace treble clef and bass clef signs:

Draw a Treble Clef:

Draw a Bass Clef:

2. Write these notes:

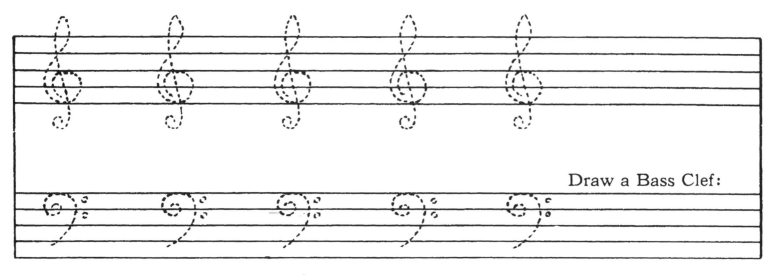

E A C G D F B	Two different G's	Two different F's

3. Notes are written on lines and in spaces. Put a small X beside each note that is on a line. Do not mark any space-notes, just the line-notes.

4. Read what the notes are saying:

 "When you are giving out the counts, I'll take one!"
(quarter-note ♩ – 1 beat)

 "Two will be just right for me."
(half-note ♩ – 2 beats)

 "Look carefully at me! Sometimes I have a dot beside me, and then I get three counts — two for me and one for the dot — that makes three!'
(dotted half-note ♩· – 3 beats)

 "That's nothing at all! I get four counts all by myself!"
(whole-note ○ – 4 beats)

5. How many counts, or beats, does each note get? Write the number beneath each note.

6. Write the counts in these measures:

THE PIANO

The piano is a wonderful solo instrument; it combines melody, harmony and rhythm, and has brilliance and expressiveness and a wide variety of tonal powers.

There are eighty-eight keys on the piano keyboard and these eighty-eight keys produce all the different tones of the full orchestra, from the very lowest notes to the highest!

The great composers have written more beautiful music for the piano than for any other instrument.

BOOK ONE
THEORY PAPER 1

Name .... Date ....

1. Here is a picture of a piano keyboard.
   Print the letter-names on the white keys:

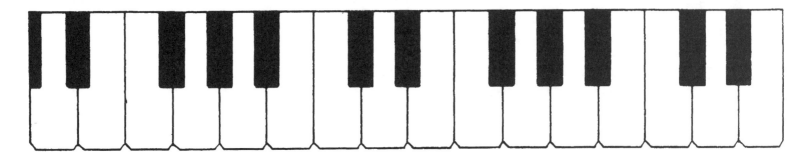

2. Write the letter-names of these notes:

Letter-names:

3. Number the fingers as they are numbered for playing the piano:

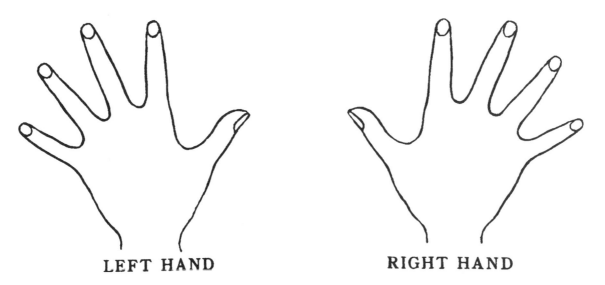

LEFT HAND　　　　　RIGHT HAND

B M. Co. 10503　　　　　　Printed in U.S.A.

TO THE TEACHER

THESE THEORY PAPERS FOR PIANO contain exercises in rhythm and notation, and are so designed that they may be used successfully with any system of teaching. The exercises are planned to resemble the problems of notation and rhythm that the beginner encounters in his first piano book.

The Theory Papers help to systematize the class written work, and to direct this important part of the class lesson towards a definite goal. The Papers add variety to the written work and are therefore valuable in sustaining the interest of the class in this work. The Papers serve as a useful check-up on the knowledge of the class, and from the written paper the teacher will be able to discover a good deal about the progress of *each pupil* in the class. This is a valuable personal contact and should be a definite help to the teacher in lesson planning. The Papers are useful as tests, or reviews. Also, they save valuable time, which every class teacher can use to advantage.

The Theory Papers are not intended to teach new musical facts, but are designed to present again—and in a novel way where possible—the facts that have already been taught, and in so doing to impress these facts on the young mind. The papers supply exercises in writing and they train the young pupil to be accurate and to observe carefully. They teach the importance of attention to each class theory lesson, since it is necessary to learn the regular lessons well in order to write the papers creditably.

DO NOT LET THE PUPIL HAVE THE WHOLE BOOK OF THEORY PAPERS AT ONCE. EACH PAPER MUST HAVE THE ADDED INTEREST OF NEWNESS. The set of papers should be kept by the teacher, each paper being given out to the class separately, whenever the class is ready to write the paper. (This will be at intervals of two, three, or four lessons, according to the progress of the class. The teacher will be able to see at a glance the knowledge that is required (notation and rhythm) to write each paper.)

The colored cover of the theory papers is separate from the set of papers. This cover is intended for the pupil to use as a holder in which to place the papers *as they are written.* This use of the cover enables the pupil to keep the written papers together in an orderly way, and adds to the pupil's interest. And the teacher will find that after the covers have been removed, the theory papers can be detached from the sets and given out to the class more speedily.

Marks may be given for the papers — or stars, or other awards. When marks are given, it should be remembered that good marks encourage the pupil and keep him interested. We generally like to do the things we are able to do well, and dislike the things, in work or in play, in which we are unsuccessful.

The sketches of musical instruments and the brief descriptions form an interesting and necessary part of the child's education in musical appreciation. Children are fascinated by the curious shapes and tonal possibilities of the various instruments. When a child has learned to know a musical instrument by sight, he will get a lasting impression of the tone color and characteristics of the instrument on hearing it played. Selected lists of records which show the tone color of the various instruments, and which are suitable for children, may be found in record catalogues. If the teacher has such recordings available, it will be very much worth while to take time to play them to the class.

The Theory Papers were intended, originally, for class work, but they may be used to good advantage in the individual piano lesson also. The beginner studying piano individually as a rule has not enough written work, sometimes almost none. The Theory Papers will interest the pupil in written work and will provide some necessary exercises. In the individual lesson the papers should be given out one at a time, as usual, and they may be written just before the piano lesson or as an assignment for home work.